GOLFaholics

by

BOB ZAHN

CCC PUBLICATIONS

Published by

CCC Publications
9725 Lurline Avenue
Chatsworth, CA 91311

Manufactured in the United States of America
Cover © 1997 CCC Publications
Interior illustrations © 1997 CCC Publications
Cover & Interior art by Bob Zahn
Cover/Interior production by Oasis Graphics
ISBN: 1-57644-041-9

If your local bookstore is out of stock, copies of this book may be obtained by mailing check or money order for $5.95 per book (plus $2.50 to cover postage and handling) to: CCC Publications; 9725 Lurline Avenue, Chatsworth, CA 91311

Pre-Publication Edition – 2/97   Fourth Printing – 2/03
First Printing – 9/97   Fifth Printing – 5/03
Second Printing – 10/98
Third Printing – 10/00

DEDICATED TO ALL THE POOR SOULS, FROM GENERATION X TO SUPER SENIOR, WHO ARE HOPELESSLY ADDICTED TO GOLF.

THIS BOOK PROBABLY CAN'T HELP ALL THE GOLFERS WHO ARE ALREADY GOLFAHOLICS, BUT IT MAY HELP THE ONES WHO ARE NOT ALREADY HOOKED, RECOGNIZE THE SYMPTOMS.

"HERE, TAKE THESE AND I'LL BE RIGHT BACK WITH MY WIFE!"

You're a *GOLFaholic* if...

YOU THINK THAT SOMEDAY YOU'LL SHOOT YOUR AGE, WHEN A MORE REALISTIC GOAL WOULD BE TO SHOOT YOUR WEIGHT.

"NORMALLY, I WOULDN'T LET A PATIENT PLAY GOLF SO SOON AFTER AN OPERATION, BUT WE DID NEED A _FOURTH_."

"IF IT DOESN'T LET UP A LITTLE BY THE TIME WE GET ON THE BACK NINE, LET'S CALL IT A DAY."

" THE POST OFFICE ?...GO A FIVE IRON WEST...
TURN RIGHT AND GO A THREE WOOD... "

IF YOU REALLY THINK ANOTHER NEW SET OF CLUBS
WOULD LOWER YOUR SCORE ...*You're a **GOLFaholic!***

"SHE THINKS I PLAY TOO MUCH GOLF!"

"HOW DO YOU EXPECT HIM TO GROW UP TO BE A PRO IF HE DOESN'T START <u>YOUNG</u>?"

You're a **GOLFaholic** if...

YOU QUIT THE GAME FOREVER,
TWICE A MONTH !

"I THOUGHT YOU SAID YOU WANTED ME TO GET THE CRAB GRASS OUT OF THE YARD!"

You're a *GOLFaholic* if...

IF YOU BUY EVERY NEW PRACTICE
GIZMO THAT COMES OUT.

"...AND THIS IS MY WORLD RECORD DIVOT
I WAS TELLING YOU ABOUT."

"CAN YOU HOLD ON A FEW MORE MINUTES? THEY'RE ON THE 18th HOLE."

"IT'S EASY TO HIT, BUT A BITCH TO PUTT!"

"IF YOU CAN'T CONTROL YOUR TEMPER, SISTER, YOU SHOULDN'T BE PLAYING THIS GAME!"

"I THINK I'D LIKE GOLF MORE IF THEY HAD CHEERLEADERS."

"I'M NOT ASKING YOU FOR A ROUGH ESTIMATE!
I WANT AN EXACT NUMBER!"

You're a GOLFaholic if...

YOU THINK YOU'RE SKILLFUL
AND EVERYBODY ELSE IS LUCKY.

"JACK'S FOURSOME GIVES OUT TROPHIES AT THE END OF THE YEAR...HE CAME IN _FOURTH_!"

HAROLD EATS LUNCH LIKE HE PLAYS GOLF.

IF YOU THINK ABOUT GOLF WHILE MAKING LOVE YOU'RE _DEFINITELY_ A **GOLFaholic!**

BRUNO HAD POWER TO BURN, BUT LITTLE FINESSE.

"A SEVENTEEN HANDICAP DOES NOT QUALIFY YOU TO PARK HERE, SIR!"

"THE PRO TOLD ME MY SCORE OF 392 IS A COURSE RECORD!"

IF YOU PRACTICED YOUR PUTTING ON YOUR WEDDING NIGHT ...*You're a GOLFaholic!*

"WHO WOULD HAVE BELIEVED IT! YOU'VE BEEN PLAYING FOR 20 YEARS AND THIS IS MY FIRST TIME...AND I BEAT YOU!"

"I DON'T REALLY CARE HOW WELL I PLAY,
I'M JUST HAPPY TO BE ABLE TO APPRECIATE
NATURE ON A BEAUTIFUL DAY LIKE THIS!"

CONCENTRATION IS THE KEY TO GOOD GOLF.

You're a GOLFaholic if...

YOU MISS THE BALL, BUT YOU STILL THINK IT WAS A GREAT SWING!

" MAN! I'VE BEEN IN SOME TOUGH SAND TRAPS BEFORE, BUT..."

"I'M SICK AND TIRED OF HEARING ABOUT THAT ROUND!"

YOU KNOW YOU'RE AN OLD **GOLFaholic** WHEN YOU START USING YOUR DRIVER TO PLAY MINI-GOLF!

"IS IT REALLY NECESSARY TO WEAR SPIKES WHEN YOU WATCH GOLF ON TV?"

You're a GOLFaholic if...

YOUR WIFE IS IN LABOR AND YOU OFFER TO DROP HER OFF AT THE HOSPITAL ON THE WAY TO THE COURSE.

"HE TOOK EIGHT SHOTS ON THE 19th HOLE!"

"YOU HAVE TO GIVE HIM CREDIT... I WOULD HAVE TAKEN THE PENALTY STROKE."

"SIT DOWN, SON, I THINK IT'S TIME YOU AND I HAVE A HEART-TO-HEART TALK ABOUT CHIPPING AND PUTTING."

...IF TAKING THE CLUB COVER OFF YOUR DRIVER MAKES YOU <u>HOT</u>!

...You're a GOLFaholic!

"WE'RE DRINKING TO OUR ROUND OF GOLF...
ONE SHOT AT A TIME."

"WILL YOU SHUT THAT DAMN THING OFF? ARNOLD PALMER IS PUTTING. SHOW A LITTLE RESPECT FOR THE <u>KING</u>!"

"I GUESS THEY DON'T TOLERATE SLOW PLAY ON THIS COURSE!"

You're a GOLFaholic if...

YOU WANT YOUR GOLFING BUDDIES TO START CALLING YOU "BEAR" OR "SHARK" OR "TIGER".

"WHEN I PLAY MY GAME I PLAY IN THE **80's**... OF COURSE,
I'VE ONLY PLAYED MY GAME <u>ONCE</u> IN THE LAST 20 YEARS."

"FRANKLY, WHEN YOU ASKED ME IF I'D LIKE TO PLAY A ROUND, THIS ISN'T WHAT I THOUGHT YOU HAD IN MIND."

IF YOU HAVE 14 PUTTERS AND YOU HOPE YOU GET ANOTHER ONE FOR YOUR BIRTHDAY ...You're a GOLFaholic!

"SEEING I ALREADY HIT YOU ONCE BEFORE, WAS I CORRECT IN YELLING EIGHT?"

You're a GOLFaholic if...

THE NEW CLUBS YOU JUST BOUGHT
COST MORE THAN YOUR MORTGAGE
AND CAR PAYMENT COMBINED!

"HE'S RIGHT...THE RULES DON'T SAY ANYTHING ABOUT IT BEING ILLEGAL TO ANCHOR YOUR PUTTER TO A NOSE-RING!"

You're a GOLFaholic if...

IT'S A 200 YARD CARRY
OVER WATER AND YOU
PLAY A <u>NEW</u> BALL !

" MUGGED ? OH, NO... I LIVE NEXT TO A GOLF COURSE."

"WHENEVER RALPH FINDS A GOLF BALL HE PUTS IT IN THE BASEMENT."

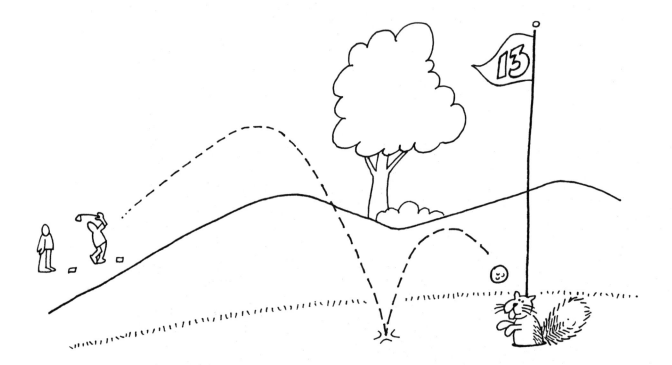

MARC WOULD NEVER KNOW HOW CLOSE HE CAME
TO MAKING A HOLE-IN-ONE THAT WARM
SUMMER DAY IN '92.

You're a *GOLFaholic* if...

YOU CAN'T BREAK 100, BUT YOU STILL THINK YOU COULD GIVE TIGER WOODS A FEW GOOD TIPS.

"I DON'T KNOW WHY YOU THINK IT'S SO HARD TO BREAK A HUNDRED! I DID IT IN _FIVE_ HOLES!"

You're a GOLFaholic if...

YOU NEVER LEARN THAT THERE ARE SOME GUYS YOU <u>CAN'T BEAT</u>!

"I'M GOING TO CUT MY SERMON SHORT THIS MORNING..."

You're a GOLFaholic if...

YOU GET TO THE GOLF COURSE AT 6 A.M. WHEN YOUR TEE TIME IS AT 10 A.M. – EVEN THOUGH THE WEATHER FORECAST IS FOR ALL DAY THUNDERSTORMS.

"I'M SURE WE'LL HEAR ABOUT HIS HOLE-IN-ONE!"

"YOU DON'T GET MUCH DISTANCE OUT OF YOUR SEX DRIVE ANYMORE EITHER!"

"YOU'RE A LOUSY LOSER, DAVE!"

THE *DREAMER*

You're a GOLFaholic if...

YOU HAVE A SON
NAMED ARNOLD.

"BY THE WAY, NO ONE HAS EVER BEATEN ME AND LIVED TO TELL ABOUT IT!"

You're a GOLFaholic if...

YOU PRACTICE YOUR SWING EVEN WHEN THE TEMPERATURE IS BELOW ZERO.

...You're a GOLFaholic if...

YOU THROW BLADES OF GRASS INTO
THE AIR TO CHECK THE WIND DIRECTION...
STUDY THE TERRAIN TO DETERMINE
THE EXACT DISTANCE TO THE HOLE...
TAKE THREE PRACTICE SWINGS...
AND THEN HIT A WORM BURNER
TWENTY YARDS INTO A WATER HAZARD!

"SO MAKE UP YOUR MIND. DO YOU WANT TO BE A GOLFAHOLIC OR A SEXAHOLIC?"

CHARLIE IS A "SCRATCH" GOLFER.

"...AND I ASSUME YOU ALSO LIKE 'OVERSIZE' GOLF CLUBS?"

" VODKA ! "

"I GUESS I SHOULD HAVE TAKEN MY GOLF COURSE MORE SERIOUSLY WHEN THEY SAID THEY WERE CRACKING DOWN ON SLOW PLAY."

IF YOU'RE MORE PASSIONATE WITH YOUR PUTTER THAN YOUR WIFE

...You're a GOLFaholic!

"I'LL CONCEDE THAT, BOSS."

"CAN'T YOU SEE I'M TOO BUSY TO TALK TO YOU?"

"I DON'T KNOW WHY, BUT I ALWAYS HAVE TROUBLE CONCENTRATING ON MY GAME WHEN I PLAY GOLF WITH YOU!"

"WHERE DO YOU THINK THIS "OVERSIZE" THING WILL END?"

You're a GOLFaholic if...

YOU KNOW THERE'S MORE TO LIFE THAN GOLF, BUT YOU'RE NOT INTERESTED IN FINDING OUT WHAT IT IS.